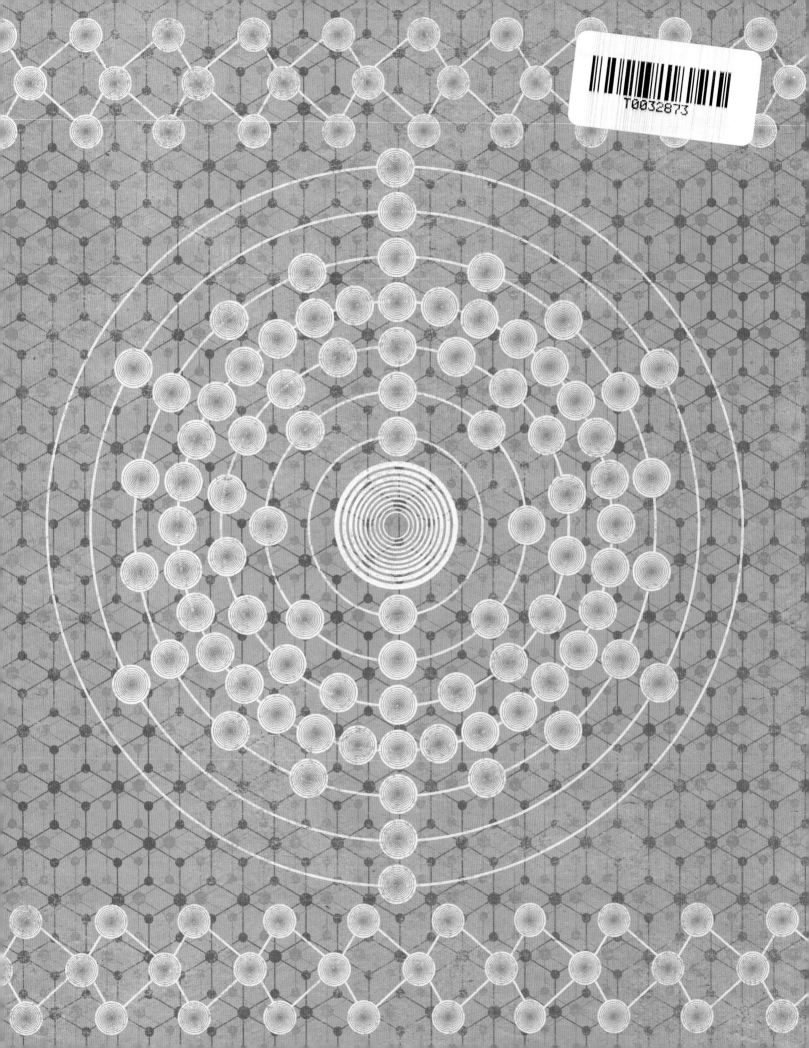

To Gabriel, Niomi, Julia, Avigail, Lyra, Talia, Leah,
Noa, Baruch, Ezra, Aviva, Orly, Ellie, David, Sarai . . .
because family is powerful! —L.E.M.

We dedicate this book to our beloved parents,
mom Albertina and dad Ennio, who follow us from
the sky with their infinite love. —A.B. & E.B.

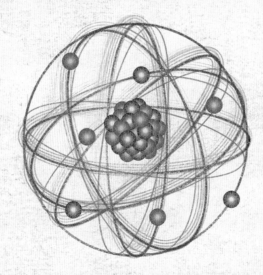

THIS IS A BORZOI BOOK PUBLISHED BY ALFRED A. KNOPF

Text copyright © 2023 by Linda Elovitz Marshall
Jacket art and interior illustrations copyright © 2023 by Anna and Elena Balbusso

Inspired by Natacha Henry's work *Marie et Bronia: Le pacte des sœurs* © Albin Michel, France, 2017

All rights reserved. Published in the United States by Alfred A. Knopf,
an imprint of Random House Children's Books, a division of Penguin Random House LLC, New York.
Knopf, Borzoi Books, and the colophon are registered trademarks of Penguin Random House LLC.

Visit us on the Web! rhcbooks.com
Educators and librarians, for a variety of teaching tools, visit us at RHTeachersLibrarians.com

Library of Congress Cataloging-in-Publication Data
Names: Marshall, Linda Elovitz, author. | Balbusso, Elena, illustrator. | Balbusso, Anna, illustrator.
Title: Sisters in science : Marie Curie, Bronia Dłuska, and the atomic power of sisterhood / Linda Elovitz Marshall ;
[illustrated by] Anna and Elena Balbusso. Description: First edition. | New York : Alfred A. Knopf, an imprint of
Random House Children's Books, a division of Penguin Random House LLC, [2023] | Audience: Ages 4–8 | Summary:
"The fascinating story of Marie Curie and her sister Bronia, two trailblazing women who worked together and made a
legendary impact on chemistry and healthcare as we know it."—Provided by publisher. Identifiers: LCCN 2022003755
(print) | LCCN 2022003756 (ebook) | ISBN 978-0-593-37758-1 (hardcover) | ISBN 978-0-593-37759-8 (library binding) |
ISBN 978-0-593-37760-4 (ebook) Subjects: LCSH: Curie, Marie, 1867–1934—Juvenile literature. |
Curie, Marie, 1867–1934—Family—Juvenile literature. | Dłuska, Bronia, 1865–1939—Juvenile literature. |
Women chemists—Poland—Biography—Juvenile literature. | Women physicians—Poland—Biography—
Juvenile literature. | Sisters—Juvenile literature.
Classification: LCC QD22.C8 M375 2023 (print) | LCC QD22.C8 (ebook) | DDC 540.92/555—dc23/eng20220321

The text of this book is set in 16-point Goudy Sans Std.
The illustrations were created using mixed media. Traditional tools
(gouache, watercolor, brush, pencil, pen, collage) were combined with digital programs.
Book design by Sarah Hokanson

MANUFACTURED IN CHINA
10 9 8 7 6 5 4 3 2 1   First Edition

SISTERS IN SCIENCE

MARIE CURIE, BRONIA DŁUSKA, AND THE ATOMIC POWER OF SISTERHOOD

BY
Linda Elovitz Marshall

ILLUSTRATED BY
Anna and Elena Balbusso

Alfred A. Knopf New York

Marie and her older sister Bronia lived with their family
in Warsaw, Poland. Their parents, both teachers, filled
their home with music, stories, and science.

But all was not well.

Their mother and a sister, Zosia, died early of illness.

Saddened, Marie and Bronia became determined to help others.

Bronia decided to become a doctor. Marie wanted to become a researcher.

But girls in Warsaw were not allowed to attend college or university.

So, Marie and Bronia taught themselves until . . .

. . . a secret university opened!

Marie, Bronia, and thousands of other young Polish women learned science, math, and the arts in private homes. To keep from being discovered, classes moved frequently from place to place. Soon the secret school was nicknamed "the Flying University"!

Yet, to achieve their dreams, Marie and Bronia needed to study in a real university, one that accepted women, like the Sorbonne in Paris, France.

But how could they *possibly* pay?

They concocted a plan:

Bronia would start at the Sorbonne immediately, while Marie would work as a tutor to pay for Bronia's education.

When Bronia finished, they would switch. Marie would start, and Bronia would pay.

Marie and Bronia made a pact!

At the Sorbonne in Paris, Bronia studied to become a doctor.

In the Polish countryside, Marie tutored children from a wealthy family.
And *(shhh . . . another secret)* although it was forbidden, she taught
peasant children to read and write!

When Bronia finished her studies, it was Marie's turn!

But Marie had changed.

She no longer wanted to study at the Sorbonne.

Instead, Marie wanted to stay in Poland with her family and friends.

But loving sisters like Bronia don't forget promises.

Bronia returned to Warsaw and reminded Marie of their dreams, their pact, and everything they both had planned.

Soon Marie was on her way.

Marie was so happy in Paris!

She had her *own* space.

From early morning to late at night, she studied physics, chemistry, and math.

She learned that absolutely *everything*—from trees to stars to water, even our own bodies—is made of teeny, invisible "building blocks" called **atoms**.

She learned that most everything is made of combinations of different types of atoms, and that some things—like helium, gold, and oxygen—are made of only *one* type of atom.

Those things—those pure forms—are called **elements**.

She learned so much . . .

and she LOVED it!

After graduation, Marie continued to work in chemistry.
For some experiments, though, she needed more space.

Bronia arranged for Marie to meet another scientist, Pierre
Curie. Pierre had designed a measuring tool that, perhaps,
Marie might find useful. He also had extra space in his lab.

Pierre and Marie met.

Soon Pierre wanted to marry Marie.

But Marie had promised to return to Poland and her father.
How could she possibly marry Pierre and stay in France?

And how could she possibly leave Pierre?
They were in love.

Bronia and her husband, both doctors and both from
Poland, had the answer. They would return to Poland to
be with their father and open a hospital there.

Marie and Pierre married . . .
and pedaled away on their bicycle honeymoon!

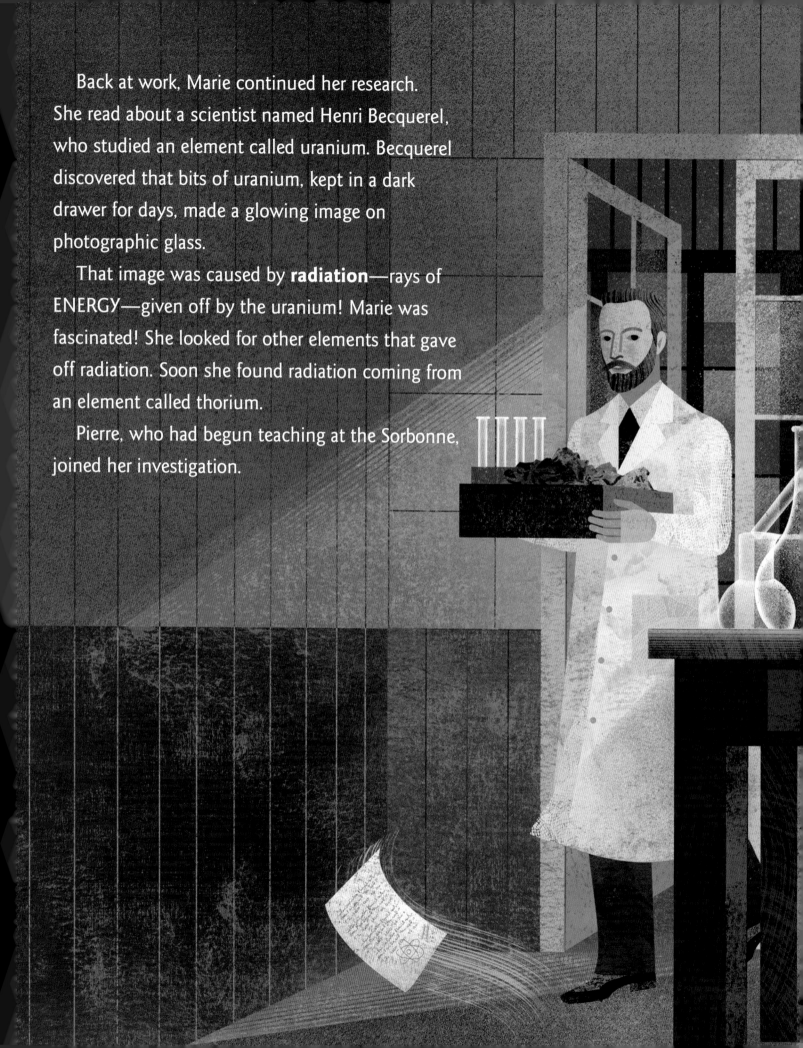

Back at work, Marie continued her research. She read about a scientist named Henri Becquerel, who studied an element called uranium. Becquerel discovered that bits of uranium, kept in a dark drawer for days, made a glowing image on photographic glass.

That image was caused by **radiation**—rays of ENERGY—given off by the uranium! Marie was fascinated! She looked for other elements that gave off radiation. Soon she found radiation coming from an element called thorium.

Pierre, who had begun teaching at the Sorbonne, joined her investigation.

Table of Elements

		Ti = 50	Zr = 90	? = 180
		V = 51	Nb = 94	Ta = 182
		Cr = 52	Mo = 96	W = 186
		Mn = 55	Rh = 104,4	Pt = 197,4
		Fe = 56	Ru = 104,4	Ir = 198
	Ni = Co = 59		Pd = 106,6	Os = 199
		Cu = 63,4	Ag = 108	Hg = 200
9,4	Mg = 24	Zn = 65,2	Cd = 112	
11	Al = 27,4	? = 68	Ur = 116	97?
12	Si =	? = 70	Sn = 118	0?
14		As = 75	Sb = 122	
		Sc = 79,4	Te = 128?	
		Br = 80	J = 127	
Li = 7		Rb = 85,4	Cs = 133	
	Ca	Sr = 87,6	Ba = 137	
		e = 92		
		95		
		118?		

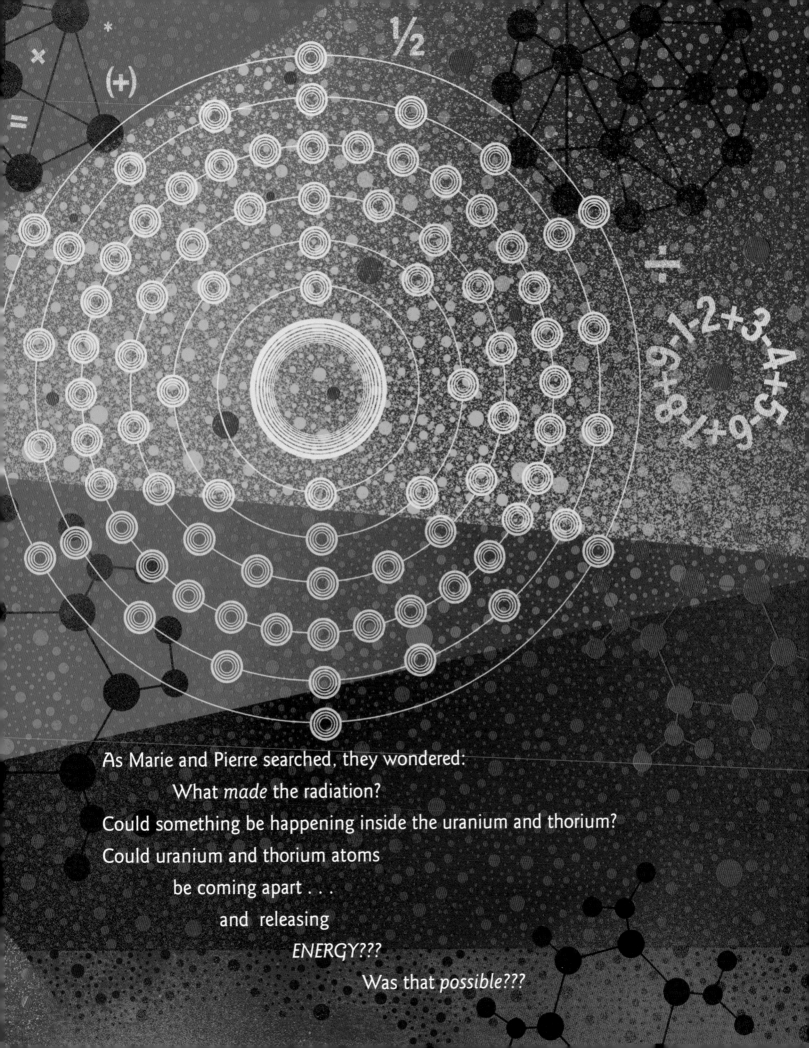

As Marie and Pierre searched, they wondered:

What *made* the radiation?

Could something be happening inside the uranium and thorium?

Could uranium and thorium atoms

be coming apart . . .

and releasing

ENERGY???

Was that *possible???*

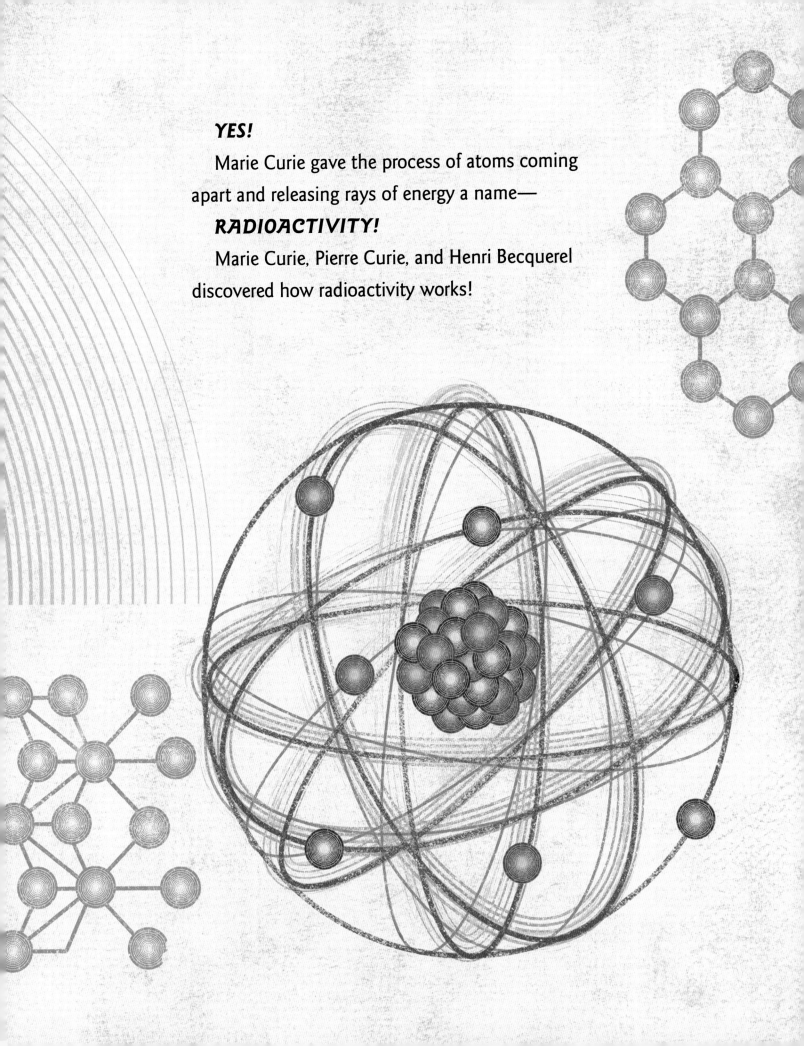

YES!

Marie Curie gave the process of atoms coming apart and releasing rays of energy a name—
RADIOACTIVITY!

Marie Curie, Pierre Curie, and Henri Becquerel discovered how radioactivity works!

Marie and Pierre searched for other sources of radioactivity, too. They investigated a dark, greasy material called uraninite. They chopped the material up. They boiled it down. They worked for years. At last, from inside the uraninite, they discovered *two* previously unknown elements!

They named the first element polonium (Po) in honor of Marie's homeland, Poland.

They named the second element radium (Ra) after the Latin word for "ray." Then they rushed to tell Bronia!

Marie Curie, Pierre Curie, and Henri Becquerel later received a Nobel Prize in Physics for their work in radioactivity. Marie Curie was the first woman ever to receive a Nobel Prize.

Marie and Pierre donated some of their Nobel Prize money to Bronia's hospital.

But once again, all was not well.

Pierre died suddenly.

Bronia hurried in from Poland!

She comforted Marie. She helped her take over Pierre's classes.

At the 650-year-old Sorbonne, Marie Curie became the FIRST female teacher!

And for discovering two new elements, Marie later received a *second* Nobel Prize.

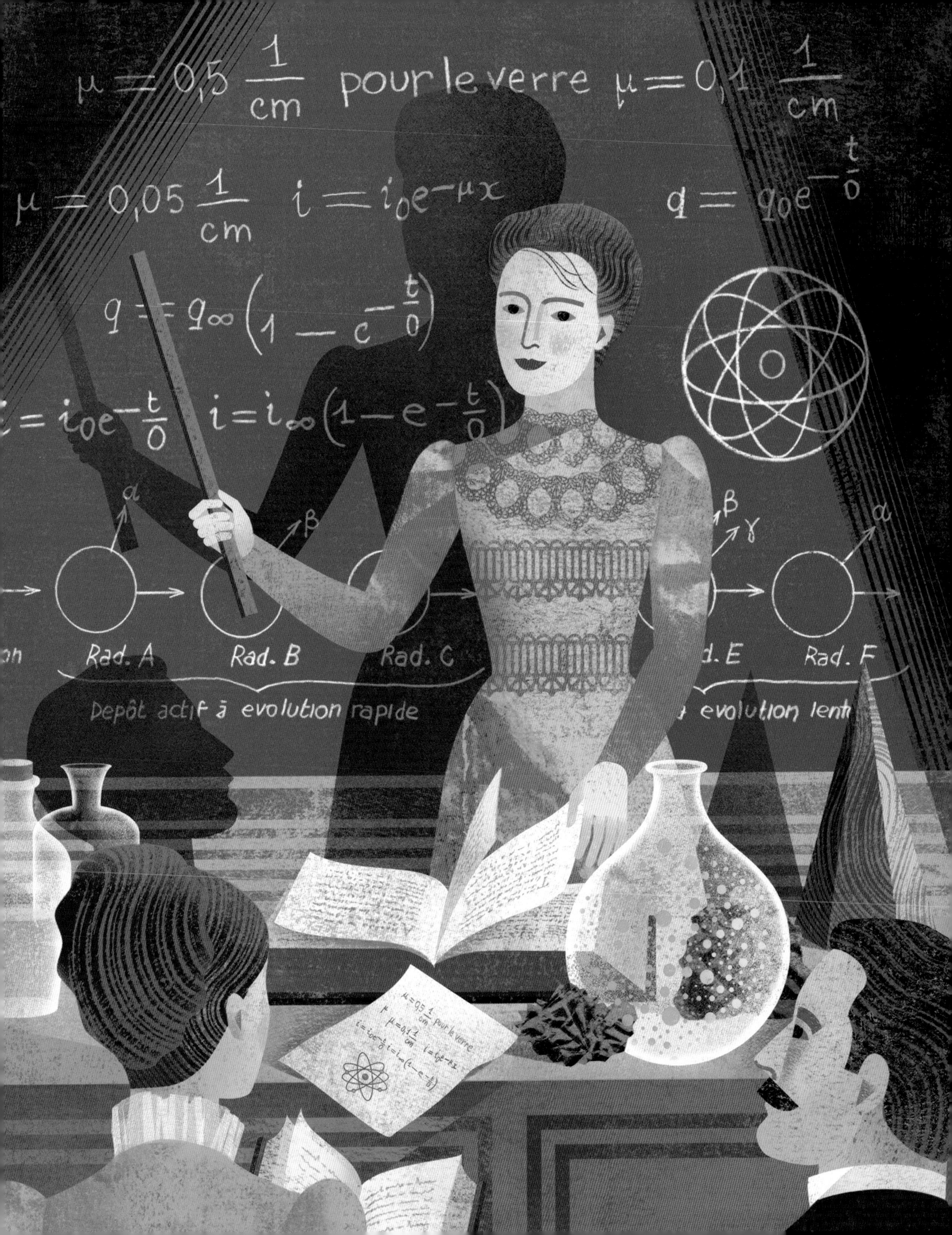
μ = 0,5 1/cm pour le verre μ = 0,1 1/cm
μ = 0,05 1/cm i = i0e−μx
q = q0e −t/0
q = q∞(1 − c −t/0)
i = i0e −t/0 i = i∞(1 − e −t/0)
α
β
β
γ
α
Rad. A
Rad. B
Rad. C
Rad. F
Depôt actif ā evolution rapide

Then war broke out.

In France, Marie developed battery-operated, portable X-ray machines. She drove them to battlefields, where the machines helped doctors to locate bullets and treat over a *million* soldiers.

Meanwhile, in Poland, soldiers received treatment in the hospital opened by Bronia and her husband.

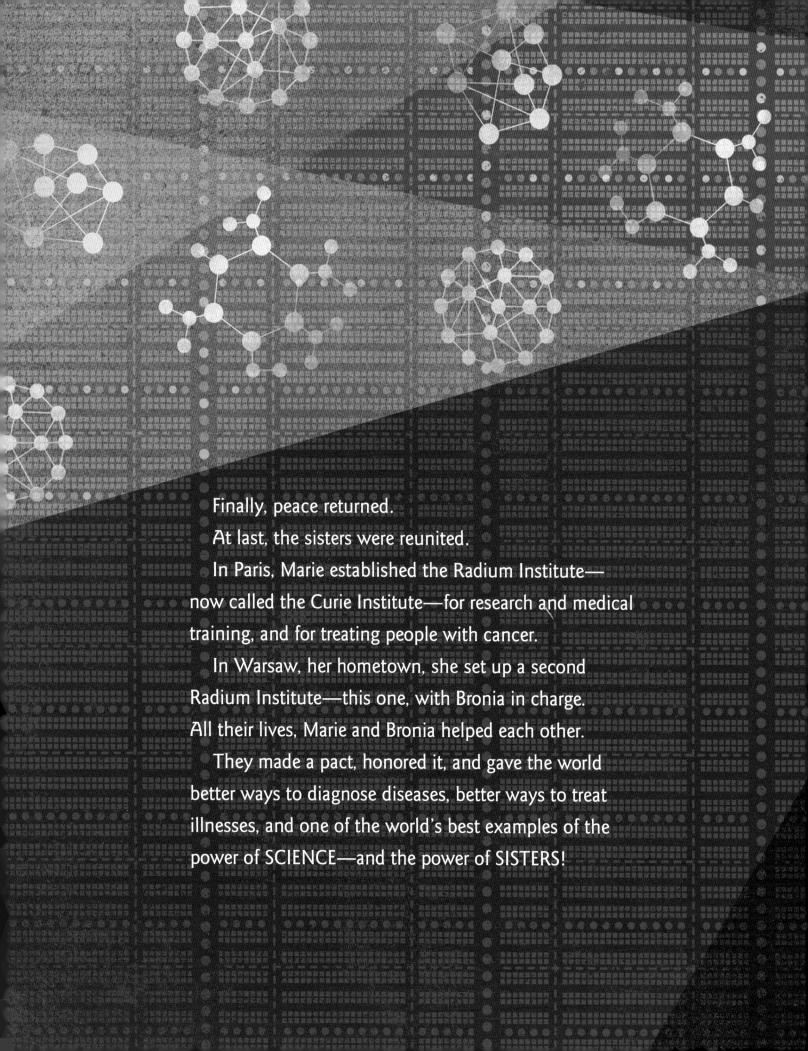

Finally, peace returned.

At last, the sisters were reunited.

In Paris, Marie established the Radium Institute—now called the Curie Institute—for research and medical training, and for treating people with cancer.

In Warsaw, her hometown, she set up a second Radium Institute—this one, with Bronia in charge. All their lives, Marie and Bronia helped each other.

They made a pact, honored it, and gave the world better ways to diagnose diseases, better ways to treat illnesses, and one of the world's best examples of the power of SCIENCE—and the power of SISTERS!

"There is nothing more wonderful than being a scientist, nowhere I would rather be than in my lab, staining up my clothes and getting paid to play." —Marie Curie

Timeline

1865 – Bronia Skłodowska is born in Warsaw, Poland. With Warsaw under Russian rule, the Skłodowski family, like many other proud Polish families, struggles to keep their Polish heritage—and language—alive.

1867 – Maria Skłodowska, the fifth and youngest child in the family, is born.

1883 – At age 15, Maria graduates from high school, first in her class.

1886 – Maria becomes a governess; Bronia enters the Sorbonne.

1891 – Maria enters the Sorbonne (and changes her name from Maria to Marie, the French form of her name).

1895 – Marie marries Pierre Curie.

1896 – Henri Becquerel notes that, left in a dark drawer, uranium produces a glowing image on a photographic glass plate.

1897 – Irène, Marie and Pierre's first child, is born.

1898 – Marie and Pierre discover polonium and radium.

1903 – Marie and Pierre, together with Henri Becquerel, win the Nobel Prize in Physics for their work on spontaneous radiation.

1904 – Ève, Marie and Pierre's second child, is born.

1906 – Pierre is killed in an accident; Bronia convinces Sorbonne administrators that Marie should teach; Marie begins teaching.

1909 – The Radium Institute, which includes the Curie Laboratory (directed by Marie Curie) and the Pasteur Laboratory, opens in Paris.

1911 – Marie wins her second Nobel Prize, this one in chemistry, for the discovery of polonium and radium.

1914 – Marie invents the portable X-ray machine; Marie and her 17-year-old daughter Irène drive the "little Curies," vehicles outfitted with radiological equipment, to battlefield hospitals where the X-ray machines help surgeons locate and extract bullets from wounded soldiers. There are 20 of these vehicles. Marie and Irène also recruit and train 150 women to operate the vehicles' X-ray machines.

1932 – Marie and Bronia open the second Radium Institute in Warsaw.

1934 – Marie dies at age 66.

1939 – Bronia dies at age 74.

Partial List of Works Consulted

BOOKS *recommended for children

Berg, Laura, and Stéphane Soularue. *Marie Curie: Grands destins de femmes*. Paris: Naïve, 2015.

*Biskup, Agnieszka. *Marie Curie: A Graphic History of the World's Most Famous Female Scientist* (Great Lives). New York: B.E.S. Publishing, 2019.

Curie, Eve. *Madame Curie: A Biography*, translated by Vincent Sheean. New York: Da Capo Press, 2001.

Curie, Marie. *Autobiographical Notes: The Story of My Life*. Paris: Musée Curie/Institut Curie, 2017.

*Demi. *Marie Curie*. New York: Henry Holt, 2018.

Goldsmith, Barbara. *Obsessive Genius: The Inner World of Marie Curie* (Great Discoveries). New York: W. W. Norton, 2005.

Henry, Natacha. *Les sœurs savantes: Marie Curie et Bronia Dluska, deux destins qui ont fait l'histoire*. Paris: La Librairie Vuibert, 2015.

Henry, Natacha. *Marie et Bronia: Le pacte des sœurs*. Paris: Albin Michel Jeunesse, 2017.

*Krull, Kathleen. *Marie Curie* (Giants of Science). New York: Viking, 2007.

Redniss, Lauren. *Radioactive: Marie & Pierre Curie: A Tale of Love and Fallout*. New York: Dey Street Books, 2015.

*Stine, Megan. *Who Was Marie Curie?* New York: Penguin Workshop, 2014.

*Thomas, Isabel, and Anke Weckmann. *Marie Curie* (Little Guides to Great Lives). London: Laurence King Publishing, 2018.

WEBSITES

artsandculture.google.com/exhibit/how-did-the-curies-measure-radioactivity-musée-curie/-QKy_qy57jACKQ?hl=en

atomicheritage.org/profile/marie-curie

Marie Curie—Facts. NobelPrize.org. Nobel Media AB 2020. Sat. 25 Jan 2020. nobelprize.org/prizes/physics/1903/marie-curie/facts/

The Nobel Prize in Chemistry 1911. NobelPrize.org. Nobel Media AB 2020. Sat. 25 Jan 2020. nobelprize.org/prizes/chemistry/1911/summary/

nobelprize.org/prizes/physics/1903/becquerel/facts/

FILMS

Mozer, Richard, director. *Marie Curie: More than Meets the Eye*. Devine Entertainment, 1997.

Rich, Richard, director. *Marie Curie* (Animated Hero Classics). Nest Family Entertainment, 1997.

PLACES TO VISIT

Link to a Marie Curie walking tour of Paris: web.pa.msu.edu/people/brock/file_sharing/ISP213H/Marie%20Curie%20Walking%20Tour.pdf

Marie (and Pierre) Curie's office and laboratory in Paris, France: musee.curie.fr/

On a Personal Note

In a way, it is *because* of Marie Curie that I began writing for children. I was in graduate school, working toward my PhD in anthropology, when an X-ray revealed a cancer. I left my PhD program and, after successful treatment, some of which was based on Marie Curie's long-ago research, returned to a deeper and earlier love—the education of young children—and then started writing for children.

Mine and countless other lives have been improved by Marie Curie. Dr. Curie's discoveries provided the basis for much of our understanding of radioactivity and radiation. From atomic power to cancer treatments to nuclear-powered submarines and spacecraft, many things in our lives are affected by Marie and Pierre's groundbreaking work.

So, the moment I heard from my friend Natacha Henry about the pact that Marie and her sister Bronia made, I *knew* I had to share the story of their special sisterhood with young people.

Thank you, Natacha, for your guidance, research, and reading draft after draft.

I hope that sisters, everywhere, will work together and, each in her own way, will help make the world a better place.

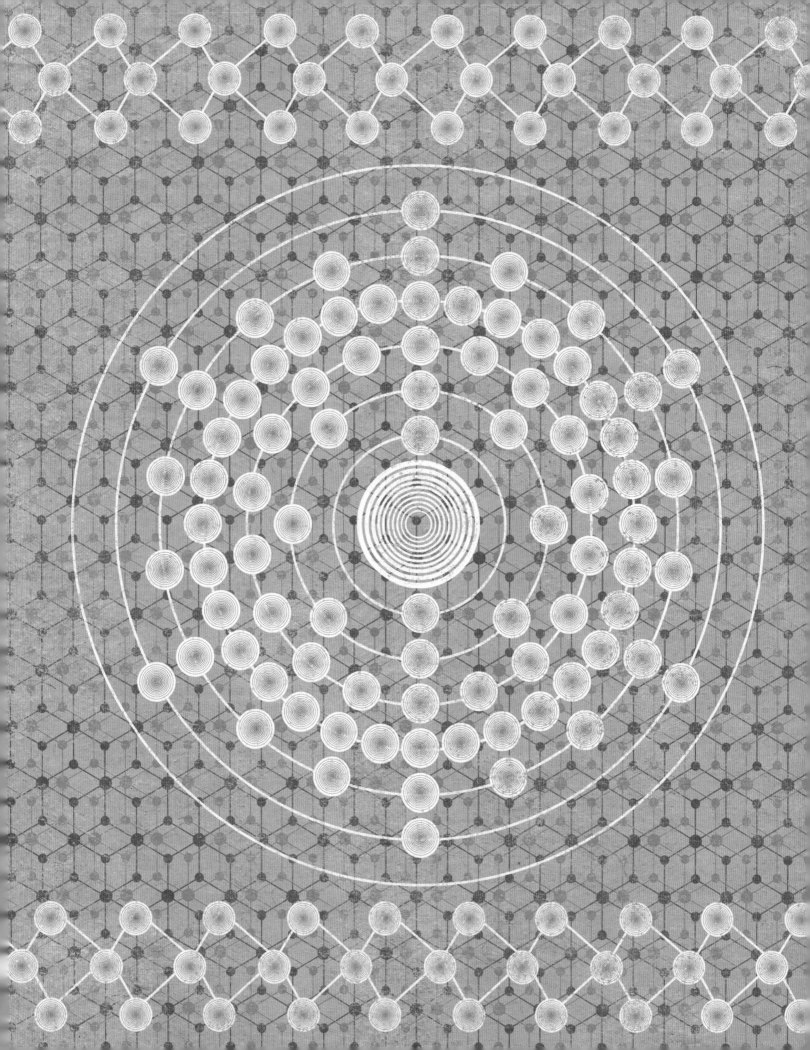